In Praise of *flaws &* "

"God has blessed Donna with using her story and the
show how God uses each of us, flaws and all, to make a difference. "Flaws & All,
You Are More Than Enough" is inspiring and encouraging—thank you, Donna, for
helping us see we are all beautiful and wonderfully made!

— Kathy Lambert, Founder, Connections to Success, St. Charles, MO

Donna Gamache is an incredible leader with a heart for serving Jesus. She
uses the gifts and passions the Lord has provided her to help others become
confidently content. Her professionalism and organization allows her clients to
feel comfortable in being transparent with their needs. She combines being a
leader in networking, business, fashion and beauty with her love for our Lord
and Savior. If you are lucky enough to work with Donna Gamache, you are truly
blessed!

— Melisa Mister, Owner of M3 Mall, Nevada County, CA

This book is a wonderful inspiration to all women who read it. As God created
all of us in His perfect image, we lose sight of our perfection throughout our lives.
I love the stories Donna has shared, showing us all that we are the same in our
struggles with our own self-image. It is God's truth we must hold in our hearts,
so our true beauty can shine. Donna, thank you for writing this very honest,
scripture-filled book. I know it will bless many women.

— Ann Carden, Business & Marketing Coach, O'Fallon, MO

Donna Gamache has a passion for helping women feel better about themselves and look better. Using scripture and stories, Donna helps everyone feel God's love.

— Karen S. Hoffman, author "Contacts, Connections & Collaboration" and founder of the non-profit Gateway to Dreams, St. Louis, MO

Donna is an expert who knows how to help her clients create a *powerful presence* from the inside out. Driven by her unwavering faith, she stands out from the rest of the "image consultants" in the marketplace because she focuses not just on making you look good, but is also committed to having you *feel* good—about who you are, what your gifts are and how to have the world take notice just by being the real, authentic you. Just as God sees you, in all your perfect design. After reading her book, you'll see the REAL you so you can stand out, stand up and experience the success you deserve—in both your life *and* business.

— Aprille Trupiano, CEO of AT International, LC | St. Louis, MO

flaws & all

You Are More Than Enough!

Donna Gamache

Lisa—
You are more
than enough
in God's
eyes —
Love —
Donna

Flaws & All

You Are More Than Enough!

Donna Gamache

Right Results Publishing

Published by Right Results Publishing, St. Louis, MO

Copyright ©2016 Donna Gamache

All rights reserved.

No part of this publication may be reproduced, stored in a retrieval system, or transmitted in any form or by any means, electronic, mechanical, photocopying, recording, scanning, or otherwise, except as permitted under Section 107 or 108 of the 1976 United States Copyright Act, without the prior written permission of the Publisher. Requests to the Publisher for permission should be addressed to Permissions Department, Right Results Publishing, donna@donnagamache.com.

Limit of Liability/Disclaimer of Warranty: While the publisher and author have used their best efforts in preparing this book, they make no representations or warranties with respect to the accuracy or completeness of the contents of this book and specifically disclaim any implied warranties of merchantability or fitness for a particular purpose. No warranty may be created or extended by sales representatives or written sales materials. The advice and strategies contained herein may not be suitable for your situation. You should consult with a professional where appropriate. Neither the publisher nor author shall be liable for any loss of profit or any other commercial damages, including but not limited to special, incidental, consequential, or other damages.

Editor: Lisbeth Tanz, LisbethTanz.com

Book design: DavisCreative.com

Library of Congress Cataloging-in-Publication Data

Library of Congress Control Number: 2016937401

Author Donna Gamache

Book Title: Flaws & All

ISBN: 978-0-9973176-0-2

Library of Congress subject headings:

   1. Contentment & Confidence   2. Faith   3. Self-Improvement

   Publication year 2016

Dedication

I want to thank many people for their support and encouragement in writing this book. I must first give thanks to my Creator, God. It is because of who He made me to be that prompts me to share on the pages that follow. Thank you, God, for being my biggest source of encouragement and my biggest supporter!

Steve Gamache, my husband, and another big supporter and encourager. Thank you for being you. I can always depend on you and your faithfulness to me and my work. Through the years, you have given me freedom to follow my passion and I am so grateful. I love you to the moon!

My sons, Max and Travis Eisenberg. You have taught me so much about life and about being me. You have loved me even when I didn't always do the right things for you as children. You have grown up to be men of integrity and faith, and I couldn't be more proud of you. Love you bunches and bunches!

Lethia Owens, my friend and Christian sister, you not only encouraged me to write this book and helped me with the title; you shared your powerful story as a contributor. Thank you so much for your continued love and support!

Lacha Hughes, Kim Manoogian, Deneen Troupe-Buitrago, Tessa Greenspan, and the Anonymous woman, I admire you and thank you for having the courage to share your story so that others may find true healing.

Finally, to my Tapestry Network Sisters (www.StLouisTapestry.com). You give me encouragement and strength to continue God's work and share with other women how we can truly be a help to one another. Thank you for teaching me to keep the faith no matter what comes.

Table of Contents

Introduction

This book is for God's glory! It is based on my experiences and those of the many women I have worked with through the years. I'm talking about our experiences of feeling broken; that something is wrong with our bodies; that we are not smart enough; or feeling we are not worthy. I wanted to write this book to address these soul-crushing experiences and feelings. I want women everywhere to know they are not alone in their feelings of brokenness.

I thought I'd heard everything until I met with a potential client recently. She shared some of the things that as a young child her mother did and said to her about her weight. I sat in shock as I listened to her explain how her mother called her fat and made her eat salad at another child's birthday party while the other kids enjoyed their burgers and fries. Her mother probably thought she was doing "the right thing" by saying and doing these things to her daughter. In reality, she left her daughter feeling wounded, unworthy, and ugly. Sadly, it was probably a behavior that this woman's mother experienced from *her* mother. This type of thinking tends to perpetuate in families…the belief that we need to be skinny and beautiful to fit in and succeed in this world.

We live in a society that demands perfection and success. Many times, perfection is defined by a perfect figure, a perfect family, or success in business. We strive for perfection, but struggle with our natural human frailties and beautiful imperfections. We struggle because of the lies we listen to everyday: "You must be perfect! You must not be flawed!" We don't or can't grasp that we are truly beautiful—flaws and all. We are created in God's image, yet perfectly, beautifully flawed with a unique purpose.

"Reckless words pierce like a sword,

but the tongue of the wise brings healing."

Proverbs 12:18

In my brokenness, I thought it was just me. *Surely, no one else is as broken as me*, I remember thinking. This perception can be very crippling and so overwhelming that we don't live our purpose; instead, we feel depleted and depressed. I pray this book will open your eyes to the reality that you are not alone in your feelings of "not being enough," whatever that means for you.

I don't consider myself an author, even though I co-authored a book and was a contributor in another one. So writing this book is definitely out of my comfort zone. Yet, I knew God wanted me to write it. I believe sharing and opening up about feeling "not enough" and unworthy will have a unique impact on each woman who reads it. I can openly say this with passion and confidence because God has called me to share my story and the stories of others so we all can learn to overcome our flaws and use them for His purpose.

After reading Beth Moore's book, *Audacious*, I was inspired to finish this book. Beth writes, "I believe God can use a book to mark a life. It doesn't even have to be a great book. It can just be well-timed. He can cause a set of pages to hit a pair of hands with the kind of timing that sparks a decision that marks a destiny. Something within those pages becomes a catalyst that shapes a calling." I believe this, not because of my great writing abilities, but because of how God can use my story and the stories of other women just like you to help heal and shape your future.

"I believe God can use a book to mark a life."

Beth Moore

We can all share in community and help one another live a life of joy and happiness amidst this crazy, out of control world we live in. I believe that as we lift one another up, we get stronger and can help others to do the same. I pray you will learn to overcome your flaws and use those flaws to help others. I pray you will learn to let go of your past and whatever keeps you from realizing just how unique and beautiful you really are!

As you read the stories of our feelings of brokenness, not feeling as if we are worthy or good enough, I pray you turn inward and consider how these stories might help you.

What has been said to you, or about you,

that has shaped your life in a negative way?

What can you do to break the bonds

of those perceptions so you can live

a full, purpose driven life?

The good news for you is this—there is healing through Jesus and God's word. There is healing through community. My deepest desire is for you to realize that you are not alone; that you can overcome your feelings of unworthiness and brokenness, to discover your purpose and share it with others. The people who need to receive your message will never hear it if you are not living your purpose. I pray this book provides you the insight and strength to take a stand for yourself and your life. You are worth it!

"For I can do everything through Christ, who gives me strength."

Philippians 4:13 (NLT)

CHAPTER ONE

We Are All Flawed

We all have fears and flaws! Even the most successful person has experienced fear. Everyone has been flawed by something that was said to them whether as a child or as an adult. So, what makes a person successful and whole in spite of his or her fears and flaws? What makes a person move forward and live for purpose instead of choosing to live a life of doubt and fear?

In these pages, I will share my personal story of being flawed by the words and actions of others and the resulting fears I have had through my teens and adult life. My story is probably not much different from your story. That is the main reason for this book. I want you to see that we are alike; flawed and imperfect, yet beautiful and full of purpose.

You will also read stories from women just like you and me. These brave women have shared childhood experiences that have shaped their view of themselves. My hope is that my story, along with the stories of these women, will encourage you to face your fears head on and live your life with purpose in spite of your flaws. In fact, I pray you let

God use those flaws to bring you closer to Him, so your purpose is revealed almost as if by magic and as a result, your message becomes bold and loud!

So let's get to the heart of it. At some point in your life, someone commented on your looks, your smarts, or something about you. I find that most of the time, it happened around fifth grade but with some it happened even earlier.

Maybe a classmate said that you were stupid or ugly or had fat legs or something else. Strangely enough, we hold onto these comments for a very long time. You would think that, as adults, we wouldn't care about what a fifth grader said many years ago. The simple truth, however, is that we do care, yet most of us don't realize it. Are you still hanging onto what was said in your youth?

A few years ago, I worked with a woman who was in her mid-fifties. She hired me to improve her overall image and identify her personal style. Based on her body shape, I knew she had great legs, so I suggested we look for a dress and skirt to round out her wardrobe. She told me she never wore skirts or dresses because she had stumpy legs. I was shocked! I asked to see her legs and, as I suspected, she had great, shapely legs. When I asked her why she thought she had stumpy legs, she told me that when she was in fifth grade, Johnny told her she had stumpy legs. This dear woman had listened and internalized what a *fifth grader* said to her and it had affected her for the majority of her life. What Johnny said in teasing (even though it was very hurtful) stuck with her for over 40 years.

I have worked with women of all ages and body shapes: skinny, overweight, tall, short—you name it. The stories are all the same. One young client kept talking about how big her thighs were. She was a beautiful young woman with a shapely body. Her thighs were not that large, but that was all she could see when she looked in the mirror. It took quite a bit of cajoling and the right outfit for her body to convince her of her beauty. As often happens, when she could finally see past her thighs, this lovely woman was almost in tears as she greeted the woman staring back at her from the mirror.

I am convinced that how a woman views her body image impacts her confidence and contentment.

Another client couldn't stop talking about her arms and how much she hated them. Another client didn't like her butt and how it looked. I could share story after story of women who don't like something about their bodies. Yet, their bodies are strong and made for them.

I truly hope that if you struggle with something you don't like about your body or yourself, that you will read on and allow my story and the stories of women who are flawed, beautiful, smart, and successful help you see that we all experience these feelings of unworthiness and not being pretty enough, smart enough, and good enough.

You are so much more than your thoughts or what others say about you. The battlefield is in your mind and heart. It is only through changing your way of thinking about yourself that there can be healing and contentment. You are chosen. You are a princess. You are God's child! God created you uniquely and divinely to be you. Embrace your flaws and use them for His glory.

"Oh yes, you shaped me first inside, then out; you formed me in my mother's womb. I thank you, High God— you're breathtaking! Body and soul, I am marvelously made! I worship in adoration—what a creation! You know me inside and out, you know every bone in my body; You know exactly how I was made, bit by bit, how I was sculpted from nothing into something."

Psalms 139:13-15 (MSG)

CHAPTER TWO

Pretty Enough

My story began when I was around ten years old (hmmm, fifth grade). I was visiting my aunt and uncle's small farm in Georgia where they raised pigs and other animals. My cousin, Teresa and I, would occasionally visit them in the summer. That summer, my outlook on the world changed all because of a comment my uncle *didn't* make.

One day, he was entertaining us by giving us rides on his shoulders. As he carried Teresa around, he kept saying how cute and pretty she was. Suddenly, it was as if I wasn't even there. I just remember wanting my uncle to say I was pretty too. I don't blame my uncle for ignoring me because he probably didn't know better. What he *didn't say* about me was just as hurtful as if he'd said something awful about me. What we say or don't say affects others, especially young children.

From that point forward, I believed I wasn't pretty. I started looking for ways to get attention so I would be noticed. I took what someone else said—or in my case, didn't say—about me as reality when it was nothing of the kind. I was a pretty cute kiddo. Yet the "not pretty" feeling led me to become insecure about my looks. I was harsher and more critical of myself from that point on. It wasn't until I was an adult that I was finally able to make peace with my uncle and myself.

I am not the only one. Successful businesswoman, Lacha Hughes, shared her story of being made fun of for a birthmark on her face and how it changed her outlook. She said, *"I have a birthmark on the side of my face. And one day, in fifth grade, I had a guy in class call me burnt face. From then on, he would bother me and call me burnt face. That made me start thinking I'm not pretty and led to low self-esteem about myself. I took the negativity that someone said about me and kept it in my head. I would always try to hide my birthmark with makeup because this one little spot had me thinking my whole face was ugly.*

"I just got myself healed about five years ago, and I'll be 44 on Thursday. So let's say roughly 28 years of dealing with the low self-esteem and thinking I'm not good enough, I'm not pretty enough, and comparing myself to other women."

Lacha is a beautiful woman with a beautiful face. You would never even know she had a birthmark, and it would not be what you would see if you looked at her. She owns two home health care agencies and co-owns an insurance agency. She is also writing her first book to share her incredible journey to healing.

"Allowing myself to know that God created me and I am who I am and there is no one like me healed me. He made me who I am and it made me stop comparing myself to other

women. It made me look at myself and say, 'I am His child'. God created me and there's no one like me so if I'm taken, then she's taken, too. I can't be like her. I can only be me. I think that I compared myself to other people, not only looks-wise but education-wise, too. I used to look at friends that were teachers, principals and had their bachelor's and master's degrees. I only had an Associate's degree, and I would always compare myself with them and think they can accomplish so much because they are educated. I could never get myself to that next level because I was always comparing myself to that next woman.

"I had a guy in class call me burnt face. That started me thinking I'm not pretty and led to low self-esteem about myself."

Lacha Hughes

"Then, I finally understood and accepted that God created each one of us perfectly. I'm perfect, and she's perfect. I am perfect because He created me that way. It's like looking at all the different flowers in the garden and knowing that's a perfect flower over there, and I'm this perfect flower here and why would I want to be any other flower?

"But as a human, I can slip back into my old way of thinking and realize that it is not just slipping back, I think it's more of when Satan sees God doing work in you, he comes and attacks you because God is trying to take you to that next level and Satan knows the weakness that you have. He tries to come in and bring you back to that level because that means you are not trusting God and believing what He says about you. The key is when you have that moment and you start dwelling on it and thinking about it, you have to snap back into reality. I do think God is trying to take you to the next level. Satan comes in saying, 'Let me take her back and remind her of how she used to be' is when God says, 'Forget about the past, the past is the past. I have created a new creature in you.'"

So many times, we feel condemned by our past, but there is a difference between self-condemnation and God's conviction. Lacha agreed: "Yes. Conviction is from God but condemnation comes straight from the devil and he loves to just get in there and mess with us. It's so true in my life.

"He made me who I am and it made me stop comparing myself to other women."

Lacha Hughes

"Most recently, I found myself pulling back from a networking group because there were so many successful women surrounding me. And the old thoughts came back...I just barely made it through high school. That is exactly when I have to stop and remember where God brought me from and where I'm at now. It is a question of facing it and saying it's a lie. I think in our brokenness, we try to hide our insecurities even from the people that are closest to us. It's because you want everybody thinking you are perfect. We don't want anyone to know the things that are going bad and that this is not right."

"For where jealousy and selfish ambition exist,

there is disorder [unrest, rebellion] and every evil thing

and morally degrading practice."

James 3:16

Another successful businesswoman in St. Louis, who chooses to stay anonymous, shared her experience of the first time she felt she was not good enough. *"I was 10. My dad took me to a soccer game because I was great at sports. When I was that age I was a little chubby. You know girls sometimes get chubby right before they start hitting puberty. I was also very athletic and was always the starter on the team. My dad was bipolar and had some issues. Even so, he loved taking me to my sporting events. After I had finished playing soccer, we went to the car. Instead of leaving, we sat in the car watching the next soccer game that was being played by a bunch of girls. Out of nowhere, my dad started laying into me. He said, 'Why can't you be like the other girls on the field? Do you see how trim they are?' He kept going on and on about my size. As a little girl, I was scared and I felt trapped because we were in the car. Where am I going to go to get away from what he was saying to me? I felt so confused because as a 10-year-old, I didn't know why he was saying this to me. It never entered my mind to think about my size. I was not even that big!*

"I discovered recently that this was the moment where I started to look at myself differently. I thought I was pretty great, but my dad wanted me to be like the other girls. I would never have even thought that.

"I felt completely confused. Here was someone who's supposed to take care of me, protect me. But I learned early that having a sick father who's not medicated meant we would see good dad and we'd see bad dad. And, you never knew which one you were going to get. So, age 10 was really the beginning of my confusion. It really was just confusion, because I had no idea what he was talking about. It's a heightened awareness at that age because until that point you're in your own little child world, but you're crossing over into puberty and looking for approval and acceptance. You're in that place where you're no longer a girl but you're not a woman. You are more vulnerable.

"This experience with my dad caused me to want to be accepted by men. Because if my dad says that I'm not good enough, then he must be right; so now I've got to prove that I am good enough in some capacity. I began seeking my identity through the approval of men

as opposed to approval of myself. I battled that on an ongoing basis until recently. It has taken 33 years to conquer those feelings. For me, the healing came through the body. I was holding all of this grief and sadness in my body. I've always been a very physical person, so my story about playing sports was just the beginning. My healing came through prayer, dance, and moving my body. I didn't know I was going to have a breakthrough the day I was at a dance workshop. There was an exercise where you look in the mirror and begin to visualize the beauty of your bones and the beauty of your body. It was like I had x-ray anatomy and could look through my body. There was a song about being beautiful playing and it triggered what's wrong with me. I realized there wasn't anything wrong with me! I actually ended up running off the dance floor and heaving tears out of my body, like I'd never experienced before. I felt like I was throwing up the grief and the emotion that was in my body. Once it all poured out, I was able to see that the grief I was holding onto needed to come out.

"I think women need to look at what makes them unique. Really get to the core of who they are. Going back to childhood and asking, 'What did I love to do when I was a child?' Was it drawing, skating, etc.? Then having her tap into the essence of who God created her to be and spending time journaling and crying over what she needs to let go of.

"For some people, it's more about spirit; for others, it is conquering the mind. For me, it was about what I felt in my body. And, I would imagine there are other women who feel the same way so it was important for me to share this with them.

"My breakthrough in my body was emphasized and helped by the exact song I needed to hear in that moment. I looked up the song and found that it is used to relieve childhood trauma. For me, it was a breakthrough and a releasing."

"I think women need to look at what makes them unique.

Really get to the core of who they are."

Anonymous

CHAPTER THREE

Smart Enough

My insecurity took me to a Christian college because of a boy rather than because of feeling confident in getting an education. I suffered a huge setback when that boy chose my girlfriend over me after we had been at college for only a semester. Whatever confidence I might have had about my looks vanished when this happened. I lost confidence in how smart I was, too. After struggling for a couple of years, I decided to drop out of school. Today, I am thankful for the time I was there and for the many things I learned that helped shape my future.

The experience with my boyfriend pushed me down a slippery slope that included drinking too much and using drugs. I felt compelled to share that bit of information here. However, that story is for another book. If you think you can't be healed because of things you did in your past, I am living proof that this is an incorrect assumption. I learned, as perhaps you have, that although I thought alcohol, drugs, and sex would make me feel prettier and happier, all of my feelings of unworthiness were still there the next morning.

He was right there waiting for me to wake up and realize that my beauty was not dependent upon what others think about me. My beauty comes from Him and from who I am inside.

It was so easy to stuff those feelings down, but one thing was certain...those feelings would always come back.

During this season of my life, I drifted far away from God. The further away I drifted, the more insecure I felt about myself. I spent many years trying to prove that I was pretty. That drift led me into some devastating relationships, which left me feeling even more unworthy and ugly. Trying to prove my self-worth and beauty through empty relationships was something I continued to pursue for years. The more I tried to convince myself and others that I was pretty, the deeper I sank into what was keeping me from a relationship with my Heavenly Father and my Creator. He is the one who always thinks of me as beautiful. I am so thankful that even when I drifted away and thought I was the one that had to prove my beauty, He never left me. He was right there waiting for me to wake up and realize that my beauty was not dependent upon what others think about me. My beauty comes from Him and from who I am *inside*.

To illustrate this self-worth pursuit another way, here is Lethia Owen's story. She struggled for years feeling not pretty or smart enough and it cost her dearly.

Lethia is the founder of Next Level Branding & Marketing, LLC and one of the brightest women I know. She truly has a gift for helping others powerfully brand themselves so they can dominate their market in business. She has come far from that self-described "skinny kid."

"I was, for a lack of better words to describe myself, a little ugly duckling. I was the little skinny kid who was all stick and bones. I didn't really know how to make my hair pretty, so I always wore two little pigtails that almost stuck straight up. Since I was a little tomboy, I never looked like the other little girls in the neighborhood. I was the one they picked to play on their team, but I wasn't the girl boys picked to say 'I like her.' That was really challenging growing up because what girl doesn't want to feel attractive or pretty? It also didn't help that I had a cousin who was very shapely and beautiful even as a little girl. She had beautiful light brown skin and long hair down her back. When you put me next to her, I was never the one that people said, 'Oh she's so pretty.' When others did say

that, I knew they weren't talking about me. My parents always said I was pretty but those are my parents and I really didn't listen to what they had to say. I wanted to hear it from somebody else. Those feelings opened me up to being very promiscuous. As I got older, I found I could get someone's attention through sex appeal.

"The one thing that was really a big eye opener for me and the thing that helped ground me was realizing I was smart when I hit high school. Until then, I didn't realize I was smart. I knew I did well in school, but I didn't know I was smart. It's interesting that once I knew I was smart, I felt more attractive. Even though nothing changed from the outside, people started to respond to me differently. People wanted to hang out with me, guys wanted to date me, because, once I felt valuable, I projected value.

"However, my promiscuous behavior led to me becoming a teenage mother. My homeroom teacher, Mr. Wilder, said something that wounded me after I told him why I was dropping out of school. He said, 'You will not amount to anything.' He spoke those words of negativity and doubt to a pregnant teenager! He also told me I would probably be on drugs or end up on welfare. His words crushed me. It was a time when I needed a lot of assurance and a supportive network to say to me, 'Hey, look, just because it happened doesn't mean it's the end of your life, so let's take the situation and turn it around.' I just needed those encouraging words but that's not what I got."

"'Hurt people,' hurt people..."

Lethia Owens

"Years later, I went back to tell Mr. Wilder what I had accomplished. I learned he had committed suicide. It was then that I realized his words to me had very little to do with who I was but more to do with who he was. 'Hurt people, hurt people.' If you're feeling low or rejected, and someone is speaking words into your life reinforcing that you are low or don't have value, it's probably because there is something within them that requires them to put you down in order for them to feel better about themselves.

"I also want to share that even though I put those feelings out of my mind and thought they went away, I still worked very, very hard for years to prove Mr. Wilder wrong. That caused me to get a reputation for being a little bit intimidating on projects in my adult workplace. This behavior was simply me showing up and trying to prove myself worthy. I was trying to prove to the people around me that I belonged there. I couldn't just show up and just be heard and contribute. I had to show up and take over.

"One day, my mentor pulled me to the side and she said, 'Hey Lethia, I really need to talk to you, can I come over to your house tonight?' I was surprised and thought, 'What? My mentor needs something from me?' My mentor had helped me so much over the years; I was so excited to be able to pour back into her life, so I couldn't wait to get together. When she arrived, I led her to my basement where I had my Bible out. I was confident that I would listen to her, read to her, help her, and support her. We settled in comfortably. What she said next I was not expecting. But it was life changing.

"She said, 'Lethia, I just want to tell you that you are enough.' I'm sure I looked surprised. I responded, 'What? Are we talking about me? I thought we are going to talk about what's going on with you.' Turns out, she had been led to tell me that I am enough. 'What do you mean?' I was still confused. She said, 'God wants you to know that you are enough. You don't have to do things for people so they will be your friend or to find value in yourself. You don't have to serve and give to people for them to value you. You are enough just being you.' I was blown away!

"Her words were the start of my liberation. I do have a servant's heart, and I used to serve because I thought that was the way to get someone to like me. Now I serve because I believe in what I am doing and in who I am. So, now it is easy for me to say, 'No, I can't do that because that doesn't work for me right now.' I still want everyone to like me; I still want to be everyone's friend, but I know if I can't support them it is OK to say so. Now

I serve from a place of power versus a place of insignificance or a lack of confidence or low self-esteem.

"The thing that makes you different, unusual, and even flawed is the very thing that makes you valuable."

Lethia Owens

"I learned that the thing that makes a woman different, unusual, and even flawed is the very thing that makes her valuable. I also want to share that what makes you valuable can also make you wealthy. When you look at your flaws, your uniqueness, and your differences through your lens, it's easy for you to see only the negative. But those are the very things that God uses and people use to identify you as different in the marketplace, in your circle of influence, and in your family. The things that make you different are the things that add your unique flavor or spice of life to the world. I call it your 'signature imprint.' It is embracing and accepting all of you for who you are. How you are wired is your 'special signature imprint.' No one else has it, and when you share it in the world, the

people who need what you have will be blessed by what you have to offer them. If you can begin to see that there's value in your 'signature imprint,' you can leverage that value and use it to help others.

"When I am in alignment with what God has created me to do, I am powerful and totally unstoppable. And, when I am out of alignment with God, there have been times when I have been crippled by fear; when I have been imprisoned by worry; and when I have been consumed with thoughts of being a failure.

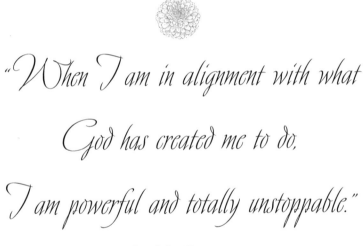

"When I am in alignment with what God has created me to do, I am powerful and totally unstoppable."

Lethia Owens

"But what's interesting is, even though nothing about my situation changes, the thing that really changes is how close I get to God and how much time I spend in His presence.

During times when I feel so connected to God and so in alignment with His will for my life, the worry, the fear, and the thoughts of failure disappear. Do they sometimes surface again? Absolutely! But I can deal with them quickly and put things back into perspective when I am spending time with God through reading His Word and prayer.

"The other thing I think is an important factor in me being able to embrace my value, be more confident, and move forward powerfully is being surrounded by other amazing women. I surround myself with women who are comfortable showing and sharing their vulnerability. Watching someone else walk gracefully through life's journey with all its pitfalls, minefields, and treacherous terrain of hills and valleys helps me to hold my head high."

"Watching someone else walk gracefully through life's journey with all its pitfalls, minefields and treacherous terrain of hills and valleys helps me to hold my head high."

Lethia Owens

It seems pervasive in our society that even today women are still given the message that they can't be or aren't smart. These messages can cause girls to "crash and burn" in school and life causing them to sabotage their success just to fit into someone else's worldview. That could have happened to Kim Manoogian. But somewhere between hunger and a strong determination to prove someone wrong, she succeeded...spectacularly.

"At 14, I was pregnant and married but it wasn't a happy marriage. My husband didn't want a divorce, and he manipulated me into staying by telling me I wasn't smart enough to ever get a job and wasn't pretty enough to ever get a boyfriend. He told me I could never

make it on my own. His cutting words were destroying my self-confidence and self-worth. Sadly, I was basing my worth on his opinion of me and justifying it because of the fact that I only had an eighth-grade education.

"As soon as my husband turned 18, he joined the Navy. We were stationed in San Diego, California, 2,000 miles away from my family and friends. We almost starved because the cost of living was so high in California. I was bound and determined to figure out a way to bring in some extra cash so we could eat.

"One day, I took the baby out for a stroller ride. During our walk, I saw these bright shiny 'Golden Arches', and I knew they were my answer. I would get a job at McDonalds. It was right across the field from our apartment. I was so excited and couldn't wait to tell my husband. As soon as he pulled into the driveway, I ran out to tell him my plan. Hardly able to catch my breath I said, 'I have a great idea, I'm going to get a job at McDonalds, I've got it all figured out, I'll work the evenings so you can watch the baby when you get home from work. It's right across the field, so I can walk' (I didn't have a driver's license at the time). He looked right into my eyes, shook his head and said, 'You are not smart enough to get a job at McDonalds. You wouldn't even be able to count the change.'

"His words stunned me, which I believe was his intent. But they did something else, too. They brought back from memory a message I received the day I found out I was pregnant. It was a defining moment. I was in the hospital undergoing testing to figure out why I was so sick. The doctor called my room to discuss the test results with me. He told me that the tests were conclusive; I was pregnant. Speechless and in shock I hung up the phone and dropped to my knees, calling out to God, 'God PLEASE help me take care of this baby, I'm just a baby myself and I'm so scared!'"

"He told me I could never make it on my own.

His cutting words were destroying

my self-confidence and self-worth."

Kim Manoogian

"I heard a voice answer my plea as clearly as if it were two people talking, 'I will take care of your son all the days of his life and in return, I want you to share your experiences with the world.'

"I looked around the room and no one was there. At this point, I was not only scared, but also now thought I was crazy. I had no idea of the message or experiences I was supposed to share. In fact, all I wanted to do was crawl under the hospital bed and hide.

"As Mark Twain so beautifully put it, 'The two most important days in our life is the day we were born and the day we find out why.'

"The day my husband told me I wasn't smart enough to get a job at McDonalds was my wakeup call and I instantly knew I had to discover why I was born, my purpose, my reason for being. It was my responsibility, as it is for all of us.

"The two most important days in our life is the day we were born and the day we find out why."

Mark Twain

"So I began a journey of self-discovery determined to figure out who I was and what I truly wanted. I knew if I was going to share my message and experiences, I had to be true

to who I was first. As I went through my discovery process, it was as if the clouds rolled away and my purpose was revealed. The discovery process I went through is a process that I created myself. I still use that exact process today with my clients.

"In the meantime, my husband couldn't accept the fact that I was becoming this new woman, and we eventually divorced. I took my first job as a waitress, but it wasn't long before I began working my way up the corporate ladder, gaining knowledge and skills along the way. I eventually became a vice president for a commercial bank. That's not too shabby for having only gone through the eighth grade. While I was still at the bank, I became a certified life coach and began coaching clients in the evenings.

"I eventually became a vice president for a commercial bank. That's not too shabby for having only gone through the eighth grade."

Kim Manoogian

"I knew I was on to something when no matter whom I worked with, a pregnant teenager, an executive, a business owner, or a blue-collar worker, if they weren't living their life designed by and aligned with who they are and what they truly want, they never felt fulfilled.

"After 11 years as a vice president of private banking, I quit my corporate job. Today I am fulfilling my passion and purpose by helping others discover how to live out their life with passion and purpose."

CHAPTER FOUR

Worthy Enough

Now, let's fast forward my life story. I met my ex-husband during my season of rebellion. We lived quite the party life for many years before I became pregnant with my first child. It was a hard time for us because, while I knew that my one desire in life had always been to be a wife and mother, he had different ideas. We had, after all, been living together for three years. He wasn't as happy as I was about having a child or getting married. However, in the end, he decided he wanted to do the right thing and we got married.

It wasn't long after having our first son that our second son was conceived. They are six days less than one year apart in age. Now the tables were turned a bit. My ex-husband was excited to have another child. After the initial shock of having a three-month-old and being pregnant, I was elated, too.

I so loved being a wife and mother to my two sons. When they were two and three, we moved to a neighborhood in Georgia where we had neighbors who were believers. They invited us to a Bible study at their home and I felt it would be the neighborly thing to do, so

I went. What I didn't realize at the time, was that God had already planned for us to live in that neighborhood with those people so that my faith in Him would be renewed.

What was hard was forgiving myself and forgetting my past. Those old feelings of unworthiness were still lurking in my mind.

God can and will use any circumstance to draw you closer. When you open your heart to Him, He will forgive and welcome you back with open arms. That is what I did after going to the neighborhood Bible study a few times. I asked him to take me back and He did. What proved harder was forgiving myself and forgetting my past. Those old feelings of unworthiness still lurked in my mind. With as much as I wanted to feel worthy of His forgiveness and love, I held onto my pain and shame for many years. What I realize now is that there is nothing I can do to be worthy; it is all about His amazing grace.

Because I was raised in the church, I wanted to raise my sons the same way. We spent many years going to every service at church, Sunday morning, Sunday night, and even Wednesday night. I sang in the choir, sang solos, was on the finance committee, did all the church decorating, and took an active role in our women's ministry. You might say I was the "church lady" and thought that was drawing me closer to God. In reality, it was just drawing me closer to the church. I thought by doing so many good things, I was making God happy with me. Can you see the pattern and how my feelings of unworthiness were still there?

What I now know is there is NOTHING I can ever do that will make God happier with me than He already is because I am His daughter. If you are a parent, you know how much you love your children. You know there is nothing they can do to make you love them more. What you want from your children is a relationship. You want to know your children and have them know you. That is exactly what God wants. He wants a relationship with you. He wants you to know Him and trust Him for everything.

What I now know is there is

NOTHING I can ever do that will make

God happier with me than He already is because

I am His daughter.

There is an old saying about "everything in its own time." I believe God works everything for us in His timing. I am not saying that He ever wants us to stray from Him but He does allow us to stray. God can use even these times of straying for His glory. He can also use our experiences for His glory. I don't regret having raised my sons in a legalistic church where they learned about God. I would, however, have preferred they be in a church that taught us what a genuine relationship with Jesus was all about. You can never go back, but you can use your experiences to draw you closer to God so you can help others.

As a wife and a mother, I gained some confidence around my looks. I was fortunate to be able to stay home with my sons and for that, I will be forever grateful! I found myself wanting more, though. I set out to find something I could do to keep myself busy and fulfilled while making some money for the family. The catch was whatever work I chose needed to allow me to continue staying home with my sons.

When I was in high school, I learned to sew and was quite good at it. I was that gal in home economics who sewed everyone's zippers for them. Recalling my sewing talent, I started a craft business creating soft-sculptured dolls. In the three years I was in business, I traveled to craft fairs in five states and employed two women part-time. Quite honestly, I didn't even know what an entrepreneur was at the time, but I was one! I ran my small business from my home, and sold over 300 dolls. I must confess that from an early age, I have had what I call "career ADD." I became bored with making dolls and moved on to (of all things) basket weaving. I must say, it is a great hobby but not a lucrative business.

You can never go back but you can use your experiences to draw you closer to God so you can help others.

My career path took a turn when my youngest son went to kindergarten. I landed a position in his school's office where I realized I had an aptitude for the computer. When we moved from Georgia to South Carolina, I secured a job as the principal's assistant in my son's new Christian school. I really honed my computer skills in that job. I also discovered I was good at graphic design and teaching others how to use the computer. Armed with my new skills, I won a job at a marketing/PR firm. While there, I created ads and taught others how to use the software. It was a rewarding time. With all my success, you would think I felt smart and accomplished, wouldn't you?

Our next move was from South Carolina to Missouri. My firm urged me to apply at one of its branches in St. Louis. So I did. However, the opportunities offered were entry level with matching low salaries. I decided to start my own company instead. That was a pretty gutsy move on my part, especially because I needed to invest in a Mac computer and the software I needed to do the work. My computer alone cost me over $5,000. My moxie paid off. Six months later, I went back to the same company that offered me only entry level positions and proposed that my company train their graphic design and word processing departments. To my delight, they accepted my proposal. I was well on my way with my business. I picked up additional clients, mainly teaching designers how to take their designs from boards to the computer. It was a very rewarding time for me. By now I should really be feeling more confident than ever about how accomplished I am, right? As always, there is more to the story.

First, let me share another woman's sense of unworthiness versus how smart she really is.

Deneen Troupe-Buitrago is a successful businesswoman with life experiences that have shaped many of her decisions about education and her career.

"At that early age, I decided I was going to be the first person in my family to go to college because then I wouldn't be like everyone else in my family. I didn't want to be in a bad marriage. I didn't want my children to have a terrible father.

"I just recently came to this realization because I was listening to an audio business book about breaking through to discover why we do the things we do and why we do it the way we do it. The book had me think back to the time when I was told something that shaped how I approached every situation since then. I remember my mother saying, 'I am surprised at you because I never thought you would make anything of yourself because you are Bob Troupe's daughter.' Hearing my mother say bad things about my dad all the time was hard on me and made me feel unworthy, since my father never lived up to his obligations. According to my mother's words, I was just like him. This made me feel like I must not be able to live up to my obligations either. The crazy thing is it pushed me to do the exact opposite of what my father did. I became an overachiever. My sisters believed my mother pushed me to excel in school, be in band, in student government, in drama class but it was thinking I was not worthy that pushed me to do so much.

"I always wanted to be a journalist like a Barbara Walters. I was on the school newspaper and on the yearbook staff and I loved it. I was accepted into a school in New Jersey for journalism and then I backed out and went to a church college that everyone goes to in our area. Because of my feelings of not being smart enough to be a journalist, I chose a safe profession. I was settling to become an educator. Now, you could say the change was a God thing. But, I believe God gave me the ambition to be a journalist, but I got scared and pulled back from it. I did get a degree and even went on to get a master's in education. I would have loved to go even further and get a PhD so I could teach college and educators.

"Because of my feelings of not being smart enough to be a journalist, I chose a safe profession."

Deneen Troupe-Buitrago

"Now, I realize I am really good at teaching. God does use us even if we don't heed His calling. Who knows if journalism would have put me in the places I needed to be? Who

knows what that life might have been like? I know it is not right to look back and 'should on myself.' That doesn't help either. What I do know is that I didn't follow my heart because of fear and doubts. I still enjoy writing and someday would like to write a book. And to this day, my mom still says things to me that make me want to doubt. I have learned to look at her and say, 'NO! You are going to stop. I am not going to listen to that anymore!'

"My mom had no self-esteem. Her father cheated on my grandmother; I am sure she was wounded as well. He also molested my mom's older sisters. It seems that kind of thing ran deep in his family. My mother was her father's favorite so, thankfully, nothing like that ever happened to her. Yet, my mother was promiscuous and in my adult years, I learned that she was also having affairs. The one thing I can really credit my father with was that he never spoke badly about my mother."

While Deneen might have allowed fear to dictate her education, she is clear about what has helped her overcome her fears and feelings of unworthiness.

"First it is God! He has been a support line to me. Even though I strayed, He was there to bring me back around and I am stronger because of it. Second is marrying my husband, Carlos. He provides us stability. Even more than being a good father to our daughters, he has allowed me to do anything I wanted to do. He's been my cheerleader for so long.

"Even though I strayed, He was there to bring me back around and I am stronger because of it."

Deeneen Troupe-Buitrago

"I realized I had to forgive my dad, mom, and stepdad for the things they did and said. Through forgiveness, I learned not to allow my past and the things that were said to me to control me. Forgiveness plays the biggest role in stepping toward healing so you can let go. It's not like those feelings, emotions, and thoughts don't creep in, but now I know that God's promises in His Word are true. God has my back and I can trust Him. He will give me what I need at the time so I can forgive. He lets me know that who I am is enough."

CHAPTER FIVE

You Are Enough

Just when I thought my life was going great, I was thrown a curveball. My first husband decided he wanted a divorce. Our marriage had not been great for a few years, but it was still a shock and something I didn't want because I knew how much God hates divorce.

Once the divorce was final, I closed my company to get a "real" job with benefits. I won't dwell on the past, but to this day, I wished I had not done that. For the next decade, I toiled as a hired consultant and worked with some of St. Louis' largest Fortune 500 companies in training and development. Consulting did allow me to make more money than ever before. I was able to support myself quite nicely. In that respect, my divorce served me well. It revealed issues in other parts of my life that I could never have foreseen.

Even today, divorce can carry a stigma. Despite my wholehearted support of my church, I learned it was not a two-way street. My divorce turned me into a pariah and I was shunned. People I had known for years turned their backs on me. This was a time when I needed my church more than ever, yet I was no longer welcome. Without a church connection, I even lost my girlfriends, whom I needed badly. Completing this sad trifecta was my abandonment of God. I was wounded both emotionally and spiritually. I chose to "go it alone."

About a year and a half after my divorce, my 46-year-old sister Vickie died suddenly of a brain aneurysm. My family and I were devastated. I took it as one more sign that God had left me. My amazing Dad died a few years later after suffering from Parkinson's disease. What a terrible disease; it took his joy of living away. His death led me to think about the years I spent in church doing what I thought was right to earn my salvation. Doing that had gotten me what? Nothing. I felt abandoned by God more than ever. What I couldn't understand at the time was that if I had truly been in a relationship with Jesus instead of just going to church doing things I thought He wanted me to do, I would have turned to God and trusted and relied on Him during this difficult season of my life. Instead, I turned my back and wanted nothing to do with Him. Over the course of the next several years, I chose to live my life the way I wanted to with no regard for God or what was really best for me.

The absolutely awesome news is that God never turned His back on me. It took me years to finally realize that it has nothing to do with what I do or my feelings of being worthy. In all honesty, I believe I could never feel worthy enough. God doesn't care. In his eyes, I am whole and complete...and totally worthy. How wonderful to have such a generous, loving support!

What I have finally come to accept is that it is by God's amazing grace and mercy that I can let go of the control and feel completely worthy because of what Jesus has done for me. He is the one who took all the sin, shame, and unworthiness of his followers upon Himself. He died on the cross so that we may live. Simply by accepting what Jesus did and asking Him into my heart, I am healed and worthy. What an amazing gift that is for all of us! Don't be like me. Don't think you have to control everything and make yourself pretty enough, smart enough, or good enough. If you have accepted what Jesus did for you, then you are already perfect in God's eyes. You can rest in that and go on to be His shining light by sharing your gifts and talents with others.

The absolutely awesome news is that God never turned His back on me. It took me years to finally realize that it has nothing to do with what I do or my feelings of being worthy.

No one exemplifies overcoming odds and doing it with grace and dignity more than Tessa Greenspan. Tessa grew up poor; rejected by a man she thought was her father. She shares how she uses the power of prayer and forgiveness to inform and enrich her life.

"When I was five years old, I found out that the man I thought was my father was not my father. He had come back from the war. When he came into the house, he picked up my sister and gave her a doll and a pearl necklace. He didn't bring me anything and didn't even acknowledge I was in the room. I went into the kitchen looking very sad. My aunt said, 'Honey, don't you worry, that's not your daddy anyway.' My mother was raped when she was 14 and became pregnant with me. Because of the day and age when it happened, she was married off to this man to give me a name. When I think back to those days, I find it incredible what one human being can do to another, especially a child.

"It was disappointing to me as a 5-year-old not to get a present but it was even more hurtful that I didn't get a hug from this man whom I thought was my father. Children want to be acknowledged and loved for who they are. I didn't get that from this man.

"Healing comes from being connected to growing and praying about everything. I literally pray about everything."

Tessa Greenspan

"I struggled with this for many, many, many years. Even though I have so much proof to the opposite, it's the one incident or two that impacts your life more than anything else. It affected me then and could still affect my confidence now. I choose not to let it by focusing on my inner Holy Spirit.

"Healing comes from being connected to praying about everything. I literally pray about everything. When I built the Sappington Farmer's Market store, I prayed about every single piece of equipment, every single item that went in that store. And that's why it was so successful.

"I encourage every woman reading this book to pray about everything. Every single day I start my day with prayer and it has made all the difference. Another thing that I always share is how important it is to forgive.

"I have lots of stories and speak about this all over the state. I recently spoke at Nelly's school (the hip hop singer from St. Louis). The kids were like, 'Oh well, she has everything together so look at what she did.' I had to tell them my background and how I lived in the Gompers. The Gompers was a section 8 housing in East St Louis, Illinois for people who were on welfare. This was where I grew up when my mother got out of the hospital after having her leg amputated because we had no money, no support system and no one who could help us. Knowing I had grown up there sure turned those students around. It was something they could relate to that provided a common ground for both of us. It's important they knew my story because it could inspire them. I say it's not where you came from; it's where you're going. It's God's grace and mercy plus our prayers that keep us going in the right direction.

"I want to talk more about forgiveness. This is really a very, very important thing for people to understand. Not forgiving will impact them negatively. When I took over the Sappington Farmer's Market, the partner giving me the keys said they were declaring bankruptcy. This was the first I heard anything about it. The previous owners left me with $413,000 in debt, which is like a million dollars in today's economy.

"This could have left me defeated and unfocused. But I knew I had to focus every ounce of energy into building this store and turning it around. And the most important thing I did was to forgive the people that had left me with this mess and debt. Now, it doesn't mean it was easy and it doesn't mean that it didn't come up every once in a while, but as it did I kept asking for grace. I kept asking God to help me let it go and help me completely forgive them. That to me was the most important part of the whole thing. If I had not forgiven them; if I would have held onto anger and hate, God would not have blessed me. Being angry and full of hate closes you to possibilities. I needed lots of options and possibilities as I tried to figure out how to pay off the debt and grow the store.

"Since I couldn't pay off the debt in one payment, I created a letter telling my creditors I would pay off so much a month till the debt was paid. By the Grace of God, little by little, I eventually paid off every single penny."

You might be wondering if Tessa was able to forgive her stepfather for his actions when she was five. She was.

"But it wasn't until years later that I forgave myself. Now I have learned to ask God to reveal to me any person dead or alive that I had something against so I can forgive them. Once I ask for forgiveness, I let it go. It is so healing. Holding onto unforgiveness just keeps us defeated and negative."

"This is really a very, very important thing for people to understand. Not forgiving will impact them negatively."

Tessa Greenspan

CHAPTER SIX

More Than Enough

The years were passing and I was still ignoring God. He, however, had not forgotten me. In fact, he led me straight to a person who has made an amazing and wonderful difference in my life—Steve Gamache, my husband.

During my years as a business owner, I did public training classes at Productivity Point International (PPI). Steve worked there full-time. I was married when we first met, so our relationship didn't go beyond the coworker stage. In fact, I didn't know him well at all. We simply went through some train-the-trainer courses together and passed one another in the hallways.

A couple of years later, I stopped training at PPI and got divorced. I still kept in touch with a few people at PPI, especially Molly, another trainer. One year, she invited me to a Christmas party she was hosting for the group at PPI. I saw it as a chance to reconnect with the people I had worked with, so I enthusiastically said "Yes!" Little did I know that night would change my life.

As I drove down Molly's street in Webster Groves, Missouri, the twinkling lights that shone from every home and the snow that sparkled like diamonds everywhere captivated me. It was truly a winter wonderland! I was so enchanted that I decided I wanted to live in Webster Groves. That decision was change number one. Change number two came as a complete surprise.

Steve was at the Christmas party that night. It didn't register with me as to how attentive he was until he gave me a second hug as I was leaving. The next day, he called Molly to ask if she thought I might go out with him. When she called to ask me, I immediately said "NO" because he is younger than I am. It was an old-fashioned way of thinking and I knew it. However, it didn't take long for me to realize that I shouldn't base my decision on age alone. When he called to ask me out, I agreed to go. We have been a couple ever since. He is an amazing and very talented man. I often call him my Renaissance man because he can do anything he puts his mind to doing. We dated for a few years, and then he proposed. There was no other answer than "YES!"

Steve and I were so happy planning our lives together and having so much fun. But in the deep recesses of my heart, I knew I needed to talk to him about God and how He would fit into our lives once we were married.

Even though I was still far away from God,
I knew I wanted to come back at some point.

We had a serious conversation about how I knew that someday I would want to reconnect with God and start going to church again. Even though I was still far away from God, I knew I wanted to come back at some point. Since Steve was raised Catholic and I was raised Baptist, we agreed that neither of those were a fit for us as a couple. We did, however, decide to start visiting churches in our area. A fortuitous invitation from my oldest son and his fiancé at the time led us to our current church. Coincidence? I don't think so...it was God's guidance.

Through the preaching and my Bible study and prayer, I am developing a real, lasting relationship with God. I love my morning devotions and lean upon Him for my strength and guidance, which feels so natural and comforting. God has also blessed me with renewed friendships from my former church. The pastor of that same church wrote me a letter asking for my forgiveness about the way he handled my divorce situation. God is so good and I am so very grateful to be able to heal those old wounds.

Steve and I have been married for 14 years as of this writing. He is my rock and even though we don't always do things perfectly, we are learning to open up and share our true feelings with one another. Communication is so very important in life, marriage, and with God.

Through the preaching and my Bible study and prayer, I am developing a real, lasting relationship with God.

We were a year into our marriage and life was great – at least at home and in church. My work life was another matter. I was still working as a corporate consultant but beginning to realize I was not being fulfilled in my purpose. One day, I came home from work and cried that my soul was dying inside me. I just couldn't work in the corporate world anymore. Steve, being the man that he is, said, "Then quit and do what you really want to do." With his support, I did two things: I applied to become the executive director for eWomenNetwork in St. Louis and started an image consulting business. On the last day of my consulting career, I learned I had been selected to be the executive director of eWomenNetwork in St. Louis (out of 24 applicants). It was also the day that I received business cards for my image consulting business.

It was through my relationships at eWomenNetwork that I met my future business partner. Together, we created an online company to help women discover and embrace their personal style. It seemed like the perfect match. I was excited to be involved in a venture that would allow me to work within my purpose, which is to help women feel confident in how they present themselves. Yet, it was in this partnership that I realized I still didn't feel smart enough. After all the years of owning my business, being a corporate consultant, directing a women's network, representing two designer lines of clothing, and walking away from a lucrative career to start another business, I still felt unworthy.

I loved managing eWomenNetwork because I was able to help women in business. I loved guiding women in finding their personal style, too. Along the way, I also became a representative for two designer lines of clothing. I am crazy like that.

Looking back, I can see exactly what happened. I allowed my partner's talk of her certifications and expertise shame me into not feeling smart enough. As you can imagine, I didn't live up to my potential in that business. After working hard for over 3 years, I left the partnership feeling drained, dumb, and financially at risk because of the money I had borrowed for the business. Wow, what a learning lesson that was! Why didn't I trust myself and what God was telling me to do? There are many reasons. I still was holding onto what others said about me and to me; I was also not in communication with God about what He says about me and wants me to do; and I was not trusting myself or my abilities. Lastly, I still thought I needed to control it all.

Don't be threatened by the talents and popularity of others.

God gifts us all in special ways.

It was during these years of directing a large women's network and co-owning an online women's style company (which turned into a boutique) that I felt the least confident about my abilities. But, as many of us do, I didn't let anyone else know I was struggling. That would be a sign of weakness! I didn't want to let people know how I was feeling about myself. I believed that if I told even one soul about how I was feeling, that person would think less of me. I was, of course, wrong about that, but when you're in the middle of a bad situation, you can tell yourself all kinds of stories. Instead, I kept everything bottled up and hidden from the world. I became an expert at "faking it." People thought I had it all together when the reality was, I was falling apart.

It took many years, many personal experiences, and the love, encouragement and support of many people for me to realize that I just needed to be myself—flaws and all. I needed to trust what God said about me and not listen to what others thought. I needed to trust that God made me the way He did and loved me unconditionally. I needed to love myself and trust myself as well.

I now know that even in the years when I felt I didn't need Him, He was still there just waiting for me to realize that I DID NEED HIM more than anything else in my life. Why do I share this with you? Because I don't want you to make the same mistakes I made. I know that I can't fix my brokenness, only God can fix it and use it for His glory. That is something to get excited about! This newfound trust in myself led me to another director position at The Tapestry Network. In this position, I bring Christian businesswomen together each month to strengthen their faith, grow their businesses, and share a sisterhood of encouragement and help. Truly, it is a work of purpose.

The more you turn from God,

the more insecure you will feel about yourself.

And this propels you to rely more on yourself

and less on God.

Through my journey of self-doubt, flaws, and fears, I have learned that those things don't define me, nor are they my reality. I have learned to trust in God for my confidence. When God empowers us, He then uses us to do His work. He selected Moses to free the Israelites from Egypt. God could have used thunderbolts to strike people dead but instead, He called on a leader, Moses, who was also a murderer. God works through people, even people who are significantly flawed. Is there a problem out there that God has called you to solve? Like Moses, you may feel inadequate but God knows you are not.

God uses your differences and

your unique signature to help others.

CHAPTER SEVEN

Confident & Content

If you ask me what makes a person confident and content, I would tell you the first step is Salvation. Have you accepted what Jesus did for you on the cross? If not, then I encourage you to start with the salvation prayer in Romans 10:8-10. First, accept God, and then believe in Jesus Christ, who died for our sins, as Lord and Savior. Then confess your sins to Him. If you are unsure of what to pray, you can use these words.

Jesus, I accept you in my heart and ask you to forgive my sins against you and against others. I ask you to save me now. In Jesus Name, Amen.

Next, make it a habit to study the Bible every day. This is God's way of speaking to you. If you read it and ask the Holy Spirit to translate for you, you will grow in God's grace. I suggest a study plan like "You Version". It is a free app you can use on your Smartphone or iPad. You can also find online plans like the "Our Daily Bread" devotionals.

Add daily prayer. This is your way of speaking directly to God and asking anything you like. He truly wants a relationship with you. He loves you more than anyone else does, so go to Him with everything. He also knows you better than anyone else...so tell him about your doubts and fears and ask Him to heal you of past hurts.

Most people make prayer something formal. That's not what God wants from you. Prayer is simply talking to God just like you would talk to your family or friends. The best way I know how to get closer to God is by getting to know each other better. If you need a good place to start, follow the example Jesus set in Matthew 6:9-13. You may know it as the "Lord's Prayer".

Here are some tips to keep in mind as you begin adding daily prayer into your life.

First, acknowledge God as Your Heavenly Father and give Him praise.

Second, ask God's will to be done. Who knows better what you need and how you should proceed in life than God?

Third, ask for forgiveness for your sins. Sin is what separates us from God. And, even though your salvation covers past, present, and future sins, unconfessed sin causes a broken relationship with God. It is the same as when you have said or done something to someone that you knew wasn't right, so you avoid the person you wronged because you feel guilty about it. Don't let unconfessed sin come between you and God.

Fourth, ask for God's divine protection from the evil one. We all need to be protected from Satan and his demons. We all need to feel safe and secure in God's love.

It is very important to find a community of believers with whom you can worship. Surround yourself with people who can support your growing faith and who want to help you grow in it. Being in a community of believers has helped me through some difficult times. Having a community of people who want to pray with you and for you is like having a favorite blanket to keep you warm. You can build relationships and discuss life's bumps and celebrations with these people.

Find a church home. Become active in attending and getting to know the other people in the church. We are not promised a completely "perfect" life after salvation. Things will still happen that cause you to stumble or maybe even derail you. Being in a Bible and Gospel oriented church with other believers will help you navigate through the good times and difficult times in life.

Here are some practical ways you can feel confident and content from the inside out.

Trust WHO YOU are in God. If you have accepted what Jesus did for you on the cross, you are God's child, His daughter. Believe it when He says you are beautiful and unique. He made you perfectly, just the way you are.

Take time every day for you. Find a quiet spot and read God's Word and pray. Find time for a bubble bath. Find time to go out with girlfriends who encourage and support you.

Know your personal style. You have a personality; it should be reflected in the way you dress. Know your personal style and then dress to impress from the inside out.

Control what you see and watch. You are in control of what you view. Only watch and read things that are encouraging and supportive.

Surround yourself with positivity. Spend time with other women who truly support you and your goals.

Don't compare yourself to others. It is so easy to fall into the compare game especially since we are bombarded with images of skinny, flawless people in magazines, on television, in movies and on social media. Focus on how unique you are and don't try to be like anyone else.

"Be Yourself, Everyone Else is Already Taken."

Oscar Wilde

Read the "Confident and Content" Manifesto daily. Say these things to yourself every day to remind you how beautiful, smart, and good enough you really are in this world.

1. I am an original.

2. I invest in myself daily by taking time to meditate on God's Word & pray.

3. I BELIEVE I am more valuable than I've ever been taught to believe.

4. I will be true to myself by knowing who I am in Christ from the Inside Out.

5. I am amazing!

6. I am imperfectly smart, pretty, and good enough.

7. I am stunning and stylish.

8. I am enough!

9. I commit to making the best first impression daily.

10. I live full out without question or apology.

11. I will not compare myself to others.

12. I trust myself and my abilities.

13. I will change my message by controlling what I listen to and watch.

14. I am savvy!

15. I am Confident and Content

16. I am beautiful, flaws and all!

I truly hope that by reading my story and the stories of other successful women, you will embrace your flaws and use them to help you break through what holds you back so you can live your life full out and with purpose.

What do you think holds you back? What attacks within your mind and heart threaten to keep you from believing in the hope of God's promise?

There is nothing standing in your way of being the smartest, prettiest, most successful woman except your flaws and fears. I encourage you to embrace them and then use them to propel you forward. You can do anything you set your mind to do.

You are more than enough in God.

Acknowledgments

I want to thank Cathy Davis for her expertise and guidance in getting this book formatted and published. She also did the front cover graphic. I will forever be grateful for your help!

I would also like to thank Lisbeth Tanz for work on editing the book and helping me make the right changes so that you got my message in a very understandable format.

About the Author

Donna Gamache has started and owned several businesses over the past couple of decades and is most proud of the work she does with women, teaching them to embrace who they are from the inside out so they are confident and content. This confidence helps women take their career or business to the next level. Donna loves helping uncover what holds them back and then helps them match their look (outside) to who they are on the inside.

Donna is a speaker, author and image strategist. It truly isn't about fashion for her, it is about defining a woman's personal style so she walks taller and is super confident in how she presents herself in life and business. Donna combines her personal experiences as an image consultant, boutique owner, representative for 3 designer lines of clothing and the work she has done with executive men and women to help entrepreneurs and professionals define their personal style so they are authentic and magnetic to prospects and clients. She has two other published books but it is her work on this book, *Flaws & All* that Donna really gets to speak her heart to women so they can avoid some of the same traps she did in her life.

Donna directed an international women's networking group for six years and is currently directing a national women's networking group, The Tapestry Network in St. Louis. She truly believes in the power of collaboration to grow and sustain business. Donna had her own radio show for over three years called the Gamache Panache radio show where she interviewed women business owners. You can still listen to the archives on blogtalkradio.com.

To contact the author, email Donna@DonnaGamache.com. To find out more about personal style, confidence and more, visit www.DonnaGamacheGlobal.com.

If you want to learn more about how to be content and confident in who you are in God, get your copy of the Confident & Content Woman 30 Day Devotional & Journal at http://donnagamacheglobal.com/confident-woman-30-day-devotional-journal/

39435423R00049

Made in the USA
San Bernardino, CA
26 September 2016